THE
GHOSTLY TALES
OF
DENVER

Published by Arcadia Children's Books
A division of Arcadia Publishing
Charleston, SC
www.arcadiapublishing.com

Spooky America is a trademark of Arcadia Publishing, Inc.

First published 2021

Manufactured in the United States

ISBN 978-1-4671-9822-6

Library of Congress Control Number: 2021938347

Notice: The information in this book is true and complete to the best of our knowledge. It is offered without guarantee on the part of the author or Arcadia Publishing. The author and Arcadia Publishing disclaim all liability in connection with the use of this book.

All images used courtesy of Shutterstock.com; p. 8 Felix Miozioznikov/Shutterstock.com; p.76 Arina P Habich/Shutterstock.com.

Spooky America

THE GHOSTLY TALES OF DENVER

SHELLI TIMMONS

Adapted from *The Haunted Heart of Denver* by Kevin Pharris

arcadia
CHILDREN'S BOOKS

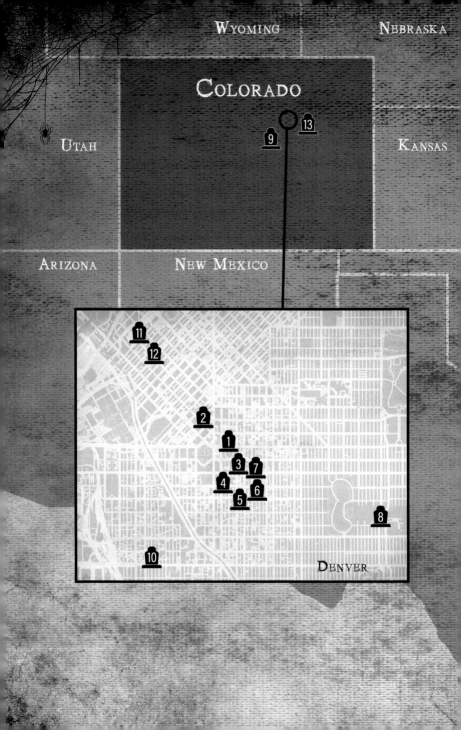

WYOMING

NEBRASKA

COLORADO

UTAH

9

13

KANSAS

ARIZONA

NEW MEXICO

11

12

2

1

3   7

4

6

5

8

10

DENVER

TABLE OF CONTENTS & MAP KEY

OKLAHOMA

TEXAS

Colorado State Capitol

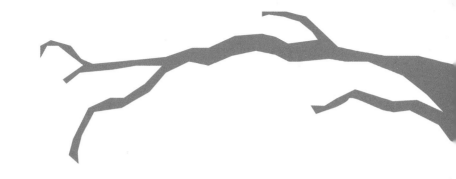

Introduction

Denver, Colorado, is known as the Mile High City due to its altitude, or elevation, of 5,280 feet above sea level—exactly one mile high. And this mile-high city has plenty of things to keep you busy. If you like sports, there are five professional teams you can root for: Denver Broncos for football, Denver Nuggets for basketball, Colorado Rockies for baseball, Colorado Avalanche for hockey, and Colorado

Rapids for soccer. The Denver Botanic Gardens offer twenty-three acres of themed gardens, and they host concerts in the summer. Denver is also known for recognizable landmarks like Union Station, the capitol building, historic hotels, and its many museums. Impressive architecture is all around, from government buildings to private homes. And of course, you can't miss the Rocky Mountains in the distance.

Denver is home to over three million people who get around by driving or taking trains or buses. It's an active city with many residents who like to cycle, jog, and walk. There are even some who just walk right through walls. That's right—the Mile High City is also home to quite a few ghosts! Denver is definitely haunted.

In the mid-1800s, people moved west across the country in search of gold. Some traveled all the way to what is now California, but others stopped to seek their fortunes along the way.

William Larimer stopped along the banks of Cherry Creek and founded Denver City. He named the settlement to honor the governor of the Kansas Territory, James Denver.

The Colorado Territory was officially formed in 1861, and Denver City felt it should be the capital. The city of Golden also wanted that honor, and for a brief period, it succeeded in becoming the capital. But thanks to a gift from a man named Henry Cordes Brown, Denver City regained the title in 1876. And with its newfound importance, Denver City shortened its name to just Denver and has remained the capital of Colorado. (Mr. Brown's gift was a piece of land offered to the Colorado Territory for the construction of a capitol building.)

That gifted piece of land owned by Mr. Brown was originally known simply as Brown's Bluff, but it soon became a very fashionable part of town known as Capitol Hill. At one point, it was even called Millionaires' Row! Nice gift, huh?

Today, Denver is the bridge between the plains and the mountains, with a heart that beats for the future but murmurs of the past, a place as beautiful as the dazzling sky above. It's no wonder that many ghosts don't want to leave.

Are you ready to meet some of these spirits from the past? Okay, then, come along with me. Right this way . . . if you dare.

Historic Home on Capitol Hill

The Corpses of
Capitol Hill

Little did Henry Cordes Brown know that the land he donated to the Colorado Territory would end up being haunted. This chapter will take you on a tour of the Capitol Hill neighborhood—a place filled with chilling stories about ghosts who have taken up residence in the most densely populated part of the state. If you follow directions well, you will be able to walk the route and see all the buildings mentioned. As far as seeing an actual ghost, we make no promises, but keep your eyes and ears open, as they are lurking out there.

THE SUMMER OF ZOMBIES
AND AN ETERNAL HEAD

Denver's nickname of the Mile High City is no exaggeration. In fact, if you make your way to the gold-domed capitol building at the corner of Colfax Avenue and Lincoln Street, you can experience that altitude quite literally.

On the west side of the capitol in downtown Denver is a famous step with these words carved into it: "One Mile Above Sea Level." If you stand on this mile-high marker, you will have a great view of the Rocky Mountains. And if you turn to look to the northwest, you will see the tall buildings that shape the city's skyline.

Among those skyscrapers, one at the corner of the Sixteenth Street Mall and Court Place stands out with the big red letters across the top that say SHERATON. From 1883 to 1933, the site where this hotel now stands was the home of the Arapahoe County Courthouse. There's nothing unusual about buildings changing names and land changing purposes over the years, but there is something very unusual about this particular location. It was once considered to be the actual Gates of Hell! Pretty wild, right?

No one is sure why it happened, but the story goes that in the summer of 1900, the elevator shafts in the basement opened . . . and the dead emerged. For six nights they walked among the guards who were on night duty, and it was reported that unnatural lights accompanied them, along with the smell of brimstone, or sulfur. (If you've never smelled it, think of rotten eggs and the stink of a skunk.)

Imagine you're just trying to stay awake in the middle of the night and do your job of guarding the place, and then, all of a sudden, the elevator doors open. A horrible stench fills your nose, unexplained lights appear, and corpses trudge off the elevator, dragging their dead bodies toward you. Clomp! Clomp! Clomp!

Who were those staggering dead? And why were they making an appearance? This was during the Wild West era, and Denver was at the heart of it. Gunfights, robberies, and murders were common. Law and order was needed, and the Arapahoe County Courthouse

helped provide it. The courthouse was where the punishment was decided for the outlaws who got caught and arrested for their crimes. Some believe that a large number of those criminals wound up in hell when they died, and when the gates opened, they escaped and returned to the site of their sentencing.

This strange and sinister event had never happened before and has not happened since, but that fateful summer of 1900 provided Denver with terrifying tales and the unique claim of access to the underworld.

Maybe it is true that spirits like to return to places where important decisions were made, especially decisions that affected them personally, such as whether they were found innocent and set free or found guilty and made to pay for their crimes. Places like jails, courthouses, and other government buildings are often home to ghosts.

As far as the capitol building itself, there is at least one ghost who calls it home. Or part of one, anyway. It's a recognizable part: his head! That's right. Just a head, floating through the capitol building. It is said to be the noggin of one of the famous Espinosa brothers from the San Luis Valley, and it was removed from his body in the 1860s.

The brothers were known as the Bloody Espinosas because of the crimes they committed. That may be a clue as to why they lost their heads. Accounts vary about whether the head of one or both brothers bobs through the hallways. Whether you see one or two, don't offer them a drink of water, okay? Unless you want to see it in a puddle on the floor after it pours out from a severed throat . . .

Wait. You're not ready to leave the tour yet, are you? Trust me, you don't want to miss what (or who) is to come . . .

THE DEVIL IN THE DETAILS

It's time to leave the capitol building and explore the surrounding area. If we walk to the south side of the capitol, we will be at the corner of Sherman Street and Fourteenth  Avenue. Walking east (away from the mountains) on Fourteenth Avenue leads toward Grant Street. Heading south on Grant Street takes us into the neighborhood of Capitol Hill. Ready or not, ghosts, here we come!

This was the area known as Millionaires' Row, remember? During the 1800s, what is now known as the Capitol Hill neighborhood was home to the city's rich and famous and their big houses. The intersection of Twelfth Avenue and Grant Street used to be called Millionaires' Corner for the spectacular homes that stood on each corner. Sadly, those four mansions are gone now, as many of the mansions from Millionaires' Row were torn down during the mid-1900s.

But luckily, some of them are still standing, including the Cresswell House at 1244 Grant Street. It is beautiful. And you guessed it—haunted!

The people who built these mansions not only wanted to show off how much money they had, they also wanted to show off how smart they were and how much they knew about the world. They incorporated elements and decorations that were used in ancient Greece and Rome into the designs of their homes.

The Cresswell House was built in 1889 for Denver businessman Joseph Cresswell, and it has had several owners over the years, many of whom added to the decorations on the outside. Some of these additions may not have been the best choices.

At the top of the house sits a stone eagle with its wings spread wide. Immediately below the eagle is a cornucopia (a symbol of plenty, usually a goat's horn overflowing with flowers, fruits, and corn) and other classical Greco-Roman images. These are all decorative and fine, but there are other items on the house that might be problematic.

At the lower corners of the roofline triangle, on either side of the eagle, are two lions that look a little like dogs. Or you might see them as dogs that look a little like lions. At the time Mr. Cresswell had the home built, people were fascinated with Asian culture and symbols, but they didn't always do enough research to properly understand and honor them. (This often happens when people use things from cultures outside their own.)

In Asian culture, these creatures are known as Fu (or Foo) dogs and, to keep things symmetrical, are always displayed in a pair, usually with one male and one female. However, the Fu dogs displayed on the Cresswell House are both male, and some say having two male Fu dogs would

disturb the building's ley lines, or energy flow, which would be a bad thing.

People may disagree about the Fu dogs affecting the energy, but there is another symbol that might cause trouble for the mansion. Between the first-floor windows is a

face that causes a lot of debate. If we consider the imagery of the ancient Greek and Roman cultures, it could be Pan, the Greek god of the wild, or Bacchus, the Roman god of wine. From Celtic culture, it could be the face of the Green Man, who symbolizes the cycle of life, death, and rebirth. But many people have gazed upon this stone face and clearly declared it to be the face of the devil!

No historical notes have been found to confirm if the face on the house was meant to honor mythology or early cultures, or to represent outright evil. The only thing certain is the Cresswell House has some strange happenings within its walls.

The Cresswell House is no longer a private residence. It is rented out as office space. But despite its beauty, the company that manages the property has a hard time keeping tenants in the building.

People who work in the building report feeling as if they are being constantly watched, and not in a friendly way. They sense someone unpleasant sneaking up behind them, planning to hurt them. Sometimes, they get an unnerving feeling that the entity creeping up on them wants to choke them to death. The feeling of dread is overwhelming, making a relaxing day at work impossible. Employees go home exhausted from being on edge all day. That mean spirit is relentless.

Was the haunting invited by the placement of any of the strange, not to mention possibly inaccurate, symbols on the outside walls? Though many people insist it is the devilish face that draws negative spirits into the home, and others are sure it is the incorrectly displayed Fu dogs that have thrown off the energy of the structure, we may never know for sure. Those items are meant to be permanently attached to the building, and removing them would not be a simple process. It also may not be easy to remove the menacing energy from the interior of the house. There is no guarantee that if the face or the animals were removed, the ghosts would go with them.

If you ever get offered a job inside the Cresswell House, watch your back. Your

coworkers may not all be among the living—
and some of them might be itching to wrap
their cold, dead fingers around your neck!

BABIES CRY AND BONES GO CRUNCH

Our next stop is 1128 Grant Street, the
imposing Peabody-Whitehead House. William
Whitehead was a doctor who came west after
the Civil War, and he was the first resident
of the home after its construction in 1889.
James Peabody was involved in Colorado
politics, which included a term as governor.
Dr. Whitehead died in the home in 1902. After
Dr. Whitehead's death, Governor Peabody and
his family moved into the mansion. Because
both men were prominent residents of Denver,
the house bears both their names. Like the
Cresswell House, the Peabody-Whitehead

house is no longer a private residence and is used as office space.

According to one ghost hunter, it is the most haunted structure he has ever entered.

It is commonly called the most haunted house in Denver. Its ghosts have been widely written about, and many séances (meetings where people try to contact the dead) have been performed there.

One Halloween, a group who was taking a tour of haunted places stopped out front, and a woman who was hosting a party invited them inside. "I'll show you around," she said. "We have the basement decorated like a graveyard."

She went on to tell the group she worked for a company on the second floor, and she and her coworker frequently saw the ghost of a toddler up there. She explained that he was a two-year-old boy and he was sad more than scary. The women had told their boss about the ghost child a couple of times, but he didn't believe them. He thought they were imagining things or trying to play a joke on him. Until he heard it for himself. One day, the boss came out of his office yelling about the crying baby that was interrupting his workday. How was he supposed to get any work done with all that crying? The women were confused at first, because no one had brought their baby into the office that day. Then they realized their boss had heard the little ghost crying. When they told him that it had to have been the ghost he heard, his attitude changed. He said never mind, he'd only been joking and hadn't really heard anything at all. Some people refuse to believe their own ears!

The leader of the ghost tour went inside the Peabody-Whitehead House that Halloween along with most of his group. They went down to the unfinished basement on rickety stairs that echoed loudly. When his foot touched the hard dirt floor of the basement, it felt more like he was stepping on something brittle and weak that shattered beneath his feet. At the same time, he heard his own voice in his mind, as if someone (or something) else was controlling his thoughts and using his voice to say, "You are not stepping on dirt. You are stepping on a field of bones."

The tour leader decided at that point he was no longer in the mood for a party, excused himself, and rushed back outside to plant his feet on solid ground. Soon, all the members from the tour group were gathered together again on the sidewalk. It didn't take any of them too long to get enough of the graveyard party in the basement or the creep factor of the whole house. They all shared things they'd felt inside. Several of them experienced pockets of

chilled air and spaces they described as having "extra gravity" or "dense air."

Could those cold, heavy areas have been vortexes, the passageways spirits use to travel between our world and what lies beyond? Whatever was coming and going in that basement felt a whole lot creepier than the toddler ghost up on the second floor.

If something took over your thoughts, bones began to break under your footsteps, and the temperature dropped suddenly, how long would you last before you hit the stairs running?

SILENT SCREAMS FROM THE PAST

As we stand outside the Peabody-Whitehead House, let's turn and look at the gigantic red mansion on the northwest corner of Grant Street and Eleventh Avenue. It was the home of Dennis Sheedy and is known as the Sheedy Mansion. And like the first two houses we've already visited, it's now an office building and no longer a private house.

While no one lives there, there is one elegant lady who relives something there.

On the north side of the Sheedy Mansion, there is a little covered entryway. Inside that door is the foyer (an entry hall or open area inside a front door). This is the spot where people often see a woman dressed in Victorian clothing. So think a long, heavy dress with layers of undergarments, lace-up ankle boots, and a fancy hat with ribbons, feathers, and flowers. Someone dressed like this today would be hard to ignore.

This woman appears to be in distress every time she is seen. Those who work in the building know this Victorian lady is a ghost. But people seeing her for the first time don't always recognize her supernatural state. Her face and hand movements exhibit panic. Her mouth moves rapidly, and she motions toward a door as if she's pleading for assistance. It seems clear she is trying to alert someone that something is wrong beyond that door. Has someone fallen, been injured, or suffered a heart attack? Most people feel the urge to help her. They rush to open the door, only to find no one there. And when they turn back around, the woman has vanished.

We may never find out what awful tragedy has upset her. Though her mouth is moving and she appears to be trying to speak, her words are not audible. She is completely silent.

Some people who study the supernatural believe she is under a thrall, which means she has been silenced for all eternity by the will of another. Others indicate she may not actually be a ghost at all. They believe there are two types of energy that can be left behind after death. Some are intelligent, with self-awareness and memory, and are able to converse with the living. Conversation may be limited by the misty barrier between our world and theirs, but they are able to communicate

with us. The other type of energy, like the woman in the foyer of the Sheedy Mansion, are not true ghosts. They are something called emotional echoes.

The idea of emotional echoes suggests that when someone experiences something terrible, the strong negative emotions of the event leave an imprint on the fabric of space, like footprints in sand. Occasionally, that imprint will surface and replay the emotions that were felt during a long-ago tragedy. Because

the woman in the foyer always does the same thing, many of Denver's ghost hunters feel she is most likely an emotional echo rather than a ghost.

What a horrible thing to repeat the same tragic seconds for all eternity. What trapped her in this painful loop? Was it her own death, or perhaps the death of someone she loved? Had she received shocking news? Unless she gains the ability to communicate with the living more effectively, we will probably never be sure what she's trying to say. Her silent screams may go on forever.

No Pets Allowed

Not all ghosts take on a visible form. Some of them are all action and no body. And some of them are such jerks it's no wonder they don't want to show their faces! The ghosts at the southwest corner of Eleventh Avenue and Pennsylvania Street are definitely not the nicest spirits on the block. But why do they behave so badly? After all, they get to haunt the very marvelous Croke-Patterson-Campbell Mansion.

Thomas Croke, a carpet dealer, had this lovely mansion built in 1891. It is in the style of a French château. In other words—a castle! Mr. Croke didn't live there long, but the mansion wasn't abandoned. It was soon purchased by Thomas Patterson, owner of the *Rocky Mountain News*. Mr. Patterson then left it to his daughter, Margaret Campbell, and her husband, Richard.

In the 1920s, the Campbells vacated the mansion for a house in a newer neighborhood. After they moved out, the mansion went through a series of structural changes, going from apartments to office space and back to a single-family home again.

During its time as apartments, the building was famous for horrible sounds coming from

a room on the northeast corner of the third floor. The mansion is known for having very anticanine energy. Whoever heard of a house that doesn't like dogs? Sadly, that seems to be the case with this mansion. Stories claim dogs have leaped out of upper-floor windows. If you know dogs, you know this is not normal behavior for them. Something had to drive them to such uncharacteristic behavior.

When one woman tried to photograph the mansion, her camera refused to work. Fearing her camera had broken, she turned to a nearby apartment building to test it. The shutter worked fine when she went to capture an image of the other building. She tried again

to get a shot of the Croke-Patterson-Campbell Mansion, but once again, her camera refused. The woman was convinced the spirits inside the mansion were preventing her camera from taking a picture of their home.

On one unseasonably hot Halloween, a ghost tour was invited into the mansion by a realtor. At this time, the mansion was unoccupied and was listed for sale. Its last resident had moved out six months earlier. Since no one was living there, the air-conditioning was turned off. And because it was unusually warm outside, it was miserably hot inside. But everyone wanted a chance to see inside the place, so in they went.

Of course, everyone wanted to check out the third-floor corner room, once known for the horrible sounds coming from behind its door. The moment the group entered the space, the temperature dropped so significantly they were all shivering in their shorts. Because ghosts are associated with cold temperatures, and given the history of this room, it seemed certain they had encountered a spirit.

Luckily, no one had a negative interaction or saw anything disturbing on that day. The cold spaces were the only signs of ghosts. And the realtor told no scary tales. But, of course, she was trying to sell a mansion, not a haunted house.

Months before, however, a tour group heard a frightening first-hand account from the prior resident. The gentleman who had lived there invited the group inside. When he was asked if he had ever experienced anything otherworldly in his home, he took them straight to a bathroom at the back of the house.

It was a large, oddly shaped room. The man stood next to the sink and told a story of the day he had been standing in that very spot, brushing his teeth, when he heard something rattling the shower curtain. "I thought it was one of the cats so I walked over there and looked in the tub," he said. "Kitty? Kitty? No cat there."

He explained that he went back to brushing his teeth, and suddenly, the shower curtain, complete with the rod it was attached to, flew across the room towards him! The man, who was a veterinarian and loved animals, also told them his cats later died in the house under mysterious circumstances.

The ghost who haunts this house will go to great lengths to let pet owners know it doesn't want to share the space with their beloved animals. Perhaps it should put up a NO PETS ALLOWED sign!

No Use Crying over Spoiled Milk

On the next block, at the corner of Twelfth Avenue and Pennsylvania Street, sits a building known today as the Pennborough. It is home to condominiums now, but it was once two separate mansions, the David Dodge House and the home of Joseph Gilluly. In the 1930s, the two houses were connected to create a hospital.

It's important to have hospitals in the community, but a hospital is only as good as its staff. This hospital once had a very bad doctor.

Dr. John Tilden had strange ideas. For example, he didn't believe germs could make you sick. Can you imagine? A doctor who didn't believe in science!

Dr. Tilden had a lot of bizarre ideas. He claimed all illnesses were the result of blood poisoning caused by an infection. He even wrote a book giving people advice on how they could cure themselves of everything from baldness to cancer. His so-called cures were not very successful. Some people think his irresponsible medical practices may have resulted in some of the ghosts who haunt the Pennborough.

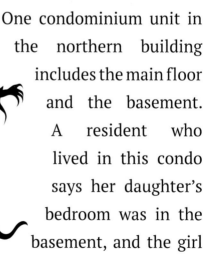

One condominium unit in the northern building includes the main floor and the basement. A resident who lived in this condo says her daughter's bedroom was in the basement, and the girl always told her parents she heard footsteps on the main floor above her room, even when she knew no one else was in the house. Her parents did not believe her. They thought she imagined the footsteps, until the girl went away to college.

The mother was in the basement one day. She was the only one home, and she heard those heavy footsteps her daughter had described. Thinking someone might have broken in, the woman ran up to the main floor. But no one was there. And this isn't the only haunted condo in the building.

A woman who lived on the second floor of the southern building claimed she had a ghost in her kitchen that liked to open the refrigerator. The spirit had no interest in closing the refrigerator door, only opening it. What a rude roommate!

Maybe the ghost liked to know what snacks were available at a glance. Maybe it wanted to feel the cool air. Maybe it just didn't understand how expensive a refrigerator full of spoiled food could be for the owner. It's not like ghosts have to go to the grocery store. Have you ever seen one pushing a shopping cart?

LET SLEEPING GHOSTS LIE

The Waring House is located at the corner of Ninth Avenue and York Street. Today, this mansion serves as the administrative offices for the Denver Botanic Gardens. It is commonly referred to as the most beautiful mansion in Denver. But behind that pretty facade are some sinister secrets . . .

In one of the offices, there is a bookshelf that holds supplies, but it also serves another purpose. The bookshelf is a secret door that leads to a small room—one that is better left alone. There is a window in the hidden room and a steep, narrow wooden staircase. The stairs lead to what was once a bedroom on the upper floor, but these stairs are not used today, and not just because they are so narrow and possibly unsafe. No, the reason these stairs are no longer used is because opening them awakens the ghosts of the Waring House.

That's right. *Opening* them is what does it. How do you open stairs? Well, these are not ordinary stairs. They can be lifted, and lifting them reveals a secret chamber underneath.

Secret doors, secret rooms, and secret passageways all sound pretty intriguing, but in this case, they lead to serious trouble. The Waring House doesn't normally show any signs of being haunted, but that is only because the spirits are usually asleep. Opening the stairs awakens and agitates them.

Once the poltergeists have been disturbed, the house experiences strange sounds, and things move around with no one around to move them. Other unsettling activities occur, too. One of these spirits may be the ghost of a young boy who died in the house. Guests on haunted tours have reported feeling their pant legs being tugged. But it seems there must be adult ghosts in the house as well, because a small boy probably isn't strong enough to push people down the stairs. No one sees the ghosts, but there is no doubt something supernatural is present and making itself known.

The activity will continue for several weeks, gradually subsiding until the ghosts settle beneath the stairs again, where they will stay until the next time someone makes the mistake of waking them up. Let them rest. They get cranky when their sleep is interrupted!

Life with Ghosts and Other Creatures

At what age do you stop being afraid of the dark? If a strange creature begins appearing to you when you're a small child lying in an enormous bed in your grandparents' farmhouse, and then keeps appearing for the rest of your life, perhaps you never stop being afraid of the dark. And you may end up being afraid of the dark again once you've read these stories...

THE REMARKABLE IVY AND HER CONNECTION TO THE SPIRIT WORLD

Let's take a little rest from all our walking. Don't worry. The ghost stories won't rest. In fact, they're going to get more personal. What follows in this story are firsthand accounts from Ivy, who lived with spirits practically her whole life. Ivy was in her early sixties when she shared these stories with local historian and tour guide Kevin Pharris. But as you will soon learn, her interactions with ghosts began in her childhood.

It all started when Ivy was nine years old, during a visit to her grandparents' farm near what is now the intersection of Simms Street and Belleview Avenue in southwest Denver. Today, this area is full of suburbs, but when Ivy was a little girl, it was farmland stretching for miles.

Ivy enjoyed visiting her grandparents on the farm. Their house had large rooms with big windows, and the bed she slept in there was not a small bed made for a child. It was

enormous, and Ivy loved to stretch out in it. When night came at the farm, the dark seemed darker than back home, and the quiet was completely silent. But she felt safe in her huge bed and believed it would protect her from any monsters.

But it was there, in that bed, that the presence Ivy would name "The Thing" first visited her. She woke suddenly one night, her instinct telling her to listen. She couldn't remember having a bad dream, but her heart raced, and she knew something was strange. Her eyes were drawn to the doorway, which was always propped open with a rock to allow cool breezes to pass through the room. That night, however, it wasn't an open door. It was an open mouth saying, "Come."

Ivy followed the voice, passing silently down the hallway, into the kitchen, and out to the yard. A presence commanded her to go beyond the gate and walk farther into the darkness. Ivy couldn't define it, but she knew something was trying to lure her away from the house. She also knew she would get in trouble with her grandparents if she obeyed it, and she feared being punished more than any creature or presence trying to control her. Shivering, she slipped back inside the house as quietly as she could and buried herself under the blankets on her big bed.

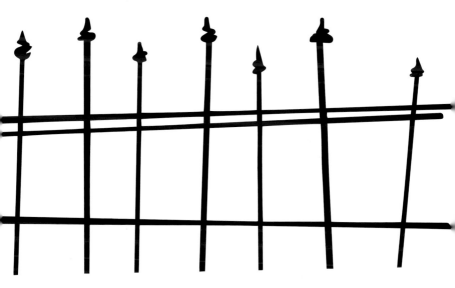

Ivy tried not to think of The Thing, knowing she would be back at home soon where nothing scary lurked in the darkness. She didn't understand then that the place doesn't always matter, and that what she feared might be capable of following her home.

A few years went by with no new interactions. But when she was thirteen, lying awake in her bed one night, Ivy heard a faint sound. She was paralyzed with fear as the sound grew, low and gravelly like a growl. A voice murmured next to her ear. At first, she couldn't understand what it was saying, but she knew it was The Thing.

Her mother came running when she heard Ivy scream. When Ivy explained she couldn't move because The Thing was holding her down and she begged for help, her mother didn't believe her. Ivy's mother thought she was trying to play a trick on her. She told her daughter to go back to sleep, turned out the light, and left her all alone in her room again. At that point, The Thing clearly said, "I will never let you go."

Ivy fought hard to break the grip of whatever was holding her. Finally, she felt a sensation like many fingers tickling her skin as they pulled away, releasing her. She turned on her bedside lamp, and when the light filled the room, she saw black ribbonlike things waving near the ceiling. They vanished a moment later.

By high school, Ivy had developed a love of watching horror movies and telling ghost stories with her friends, but she still feared The Thing. She was never sure if she had opened her mind to the negative spirit or if it had forced its way in, but after its arrival, she saw glimpses from the other side almost everywhere she went.

One summer night, she and three friends drove to Red Rocks to search for the legendary Hatchet Lady, a headless ghost who rides horseback, swinging a bloody hatchet. Knowing it might only be an urban myth didn't make the adventure any less exciting. The park was darker back then than it is today, because the lights of the city weren't so close. Ivy and her friends parked and headed for the high rock formations.

A glowing white ball of light suddenly appeared on the east rock face. Ivy was the first to see it. There was no source for the light, but it expanded and brightened. They decided they didn't need to see the Hatchet Lady after all and left in a hurry. Whatever had greeted them in the form of that glowing orb was enough of a thrill for one night.

For a while, Ivy's parents had a standing threefold mirror in their bedroom. The center section was stationary, but the two sections on either side could be repositioned. Ivy liked to stand with the outer mirrors angled toward her, seeing herself reflected into infinity. Later, her father disassembled the mirror, keeping only the center section and adding hooks for coats and a drawer for gloves. He moved it to the hallway.

Even without the side mirrors adding dimension to the reflection, Ivy felt this mirror still looked deeper than others. She realized she was right when she began to see a woman wearing a long, brown dress in the mirror. The woman appeared to be in her thirties, and she wore her brown hair in a bun high on top of her head. She didn't stare out at Ivy from the mirror but seemed to be standing in front of it looking at her own reflection, just as Ivy liked to do.

Sometimes, Ivy would only catch part of the woman in the mirror, as if she'd been looking at herself and Ivy's approach caused her to leave. Many times, only the back of the woman was visible as she walked away, deeper into the mirror.

One day, Ivy casually asked her father where he had gotten the mirror. Was it a family heirloom? Did he know anything about its history? His answer was disappointing. He had found the mirror in a salvage shop, discarded and forgotten. There was no way to trace the mirror back to the lady Ivy saw in its depths. The mirror still stands in the same spot, but the lady in the brown dress has never returned.

Her home wasn't the only place Ivy encountered ghosts. When she was in the eighth grade, Ivy went with a group of her

friends to visit a mansion in Capitol Hill that had belonged to Charles Boettcher Jr. at 777 Washington Street. The house had been long abandoned by the time Ivy and her friends went exploring, hoping to confirm it was truly haunted. (This old Boettcher mansion still stands, but it is now Governor's Park Condominiums.)

The mother of one of the girls drove them. Their main goal was to check out an upstairs bathroom where a murder had occurred. At least, that is what they had been told.

Ivy and her friends entered the house through an open side door. The Boettchers were one of the great families of Denver's history, and at one time, they owned many houses. The furniture had all been removed from the house on Washington Street, and several of the walls had been torn open, revealing pipes and boards. Broken glass covered the stairs, and it cracked beneath their feet as they walked up to the second floor.

All the girls found upstairs was pigeons and something smeared on a bathroom wall that they convinced themselves could have been blood. It was enough to satisfy their curiosity. They huddled together as they walked back down the stairs, chatting about what they'd seen.

A burst of laughter startled them. They turned together to see who was there, and saw a pale figure standing at the top of the stairs, barely six feet behind them. He was tall and

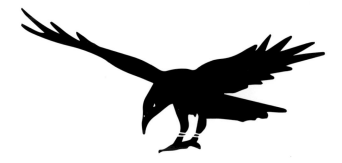

thin, wore a long black cape, and he glared at them with bulging eyes.

The girls froze, and the figure's voice came out high like a flute, as if it were carried on racing winds. "Did you enjoy your stay?" His voice was funny, but nothing about his face was humorous. He started laughing at them again, and the girls fled the house as quickly as they could.

By the time Ivy was twenty-two, she was married and had two daughters. When her parents moved to the mountains, Ivy and her husband bought the house where she'd grown up and moved in with their young family. And the ghosts kept coming.

One day Ivy was visiting with some friends in her kitchen. They were discussing the paranormal, and her friends agreed they would love to see a ghost. Her friends weren't content to see only unexplained things that might be caused by a spirit. They wanted to be absolutely certain that had seen the form of a ghost. Ivy kept silent, but the words had been spoken, and once spoken, words can't be taken back. From where she sat, Ivy could see past her friends to the hallway. A ghost stepped from a bedroom to fulfill her friends' request.

His appearance was not welcomed by Ivy. She described seeing him walk through the closed door. He appeared as thousands of moving particles working together to form his image. There were no colors, but she could see patterns: a checkered flannel shirt, heavy pants, and suspenders. He looked toward the kitchen and continued moving in their direction.

Watching him walk was upsetting to Ivy. His movements were jerky, and his joints didn't always bend in the right direction—his knees and elbows could bend backward. His eyes were wide, and his head lolled from side to side with each horrible lurch forward. Ivy's friends heard her catch her breath and turned to see what she was staring at. They were as horrified as Ivy when they saw what had startled her.

Fortunately, the ghost walked into the bathroom instead of continuing their way.

The group raced to the spot in the hallway where they'd seen him. The air was cold as a freezer. They could move their hands into and out of the temperature difference in the space. They found no signs of the ghost in the bathroom. Ivy's friends who had wanted to see a ghost admitted he was not what they expected. It had been more frightening than exciting.

Ivy warned them not to wish for such a thing ever again.

The vision of that broken man haunted Ivy's dreams for a long time to come. And voices began to interrupt her nights as well.

Sometimes a male voice would call her name, waking her from a sound sleep. No one else ever heard the voice. It was always the same, low and clear but not threatening. Ivy decided someone wanted to make her aware that she was not alone.

The voice that came to her in the night seemed harmless enough, but Ivy couldn't help but wonder if it was associated with the lurching man whom she and her friends had seen in her hallway. Had he been The Thing?

Over the years, The Thing visited Ivy less and less. She believes her children brought great strength into the home, and the positive energy of all of them together kept the force away. After her children grew up and moved away, leaving Ivy to live alone in her house, The Thing's visits became more frequent again, but her fear wasn't so powerful anymore. He was the first spirit to bother Ivy, but he certainly wasn't the last.

Can you imagine having to deal with ghosts and strange supernatural beings your whole life? You might never outgrow being afraid of the dark. I don't think I would ever turn off the lights . . .

An Infestation on Inca Street

A married couple named Brinker and Stella decided to buy a house on Inca Street in the Greater Baker neighborhood. The area was being revitalized, and it seemed like a great investment. They felt enthusiastic about the remodeling project, but they knew it would take a lot of work to restore the house.

The front yard was nothing but weeds and dirt, and the backyard had been completely covered with cement. In terms of the house, the upstairs was only partially finished, and the main floor was an odd assortment of doors in confusing places and walls where they didn't belong. The kitchen alone had four different doorways and a stairwell.

Right away, Stella felt uneasy in the house. It didn't help that her husband, Brinker, had to be away for work. While he was gone, Stella had trouble sleeping. She began hearing strange noises coming from the unfinished rooms upstairs.

When Brinker was home, the couple went upstairs together to see if they could find the source of the skittering noises Stella had heard. She expected to find tiny footprints in the dust, the kind made by mice or squirrels. There were no signs of animals at all. What else could have made those noises she heard?

The next time Brinker was out of town for work, the noises returned. There was no mistaking it was the sound of small feet moving across the upstairs floor. Stella found the courage to grab a flashlight and go up to the second floor on her own to investigate. Once again, she saw no signs of animals or anything else to explain the sounds. But then, she heard the sound of multiple small feet moving down the stairs.

Stella described it as sounding kind of like a dog walking on hardwood floors with its nails clicking against the surface. But the sounds she heard were softer, as if they'd been made by a smaller animal. When she got down to the main floor, she saw nothing to explain the noises. She turned on all the lights and searched everywhere, but she found nothing.

Things got weirder in the house after that night she went upstairs alone. If Stella left the door open to bring in groceries, stray cats would rush into the house. Brinker is allergic to almost every animal, so they had to get them out, but it was nearly impossible. The cats would hiss, hide behind furniture, scratch, and bite.

Cats weren't the only animals that came inside. Squirrels would bite through screens. Mice found openings all over the old house. Every type of insect began to invade their home, especially spiders. They even found a couple of black widows!

They hired exterminators to get rid of the insects, but no amount of spraying was enough. No matter how many times they had the screens repaired or patched up holes, the squirrels and mice kept getting in, and the cats wouldn't stay out.

Eventually, Brinker and Stella moved out of the house. They kept it, thinking they could still fix it up and sell it. One day when they returned to the house to do some work, it was full of dead insects. And that wasn't all. There were dead mice everywhere, a dead squirrel, and a dead pigeon just outside a window.

Stella always felt she may have disturbed some restless spirits by going upstairs. She wasn't sure if it was the ghost of a person or an animal, or even many ghosts. Whatever it was definitely attracted the cats to the house and agitated them to the point of hissing, scratching, and biting. It drew thousands of creeping spiders and bugs. The skittering claws and chewing teeth of mice and squirrels responded to the call as if they'd been possessed to get inside.

On the advice of a friend, Brinker and Stella set out papers with a specially drawn maze. The maze had no exits, and the idea was that it would draw the ghosts in and trap them. Brinker and Stella were skeptical, but they wanted the ghosts gone, so they placed a copy of the maze on each floor of the house and left them there for two months. When they returned, there were no dead animals, and no new damages to the house. The papers were covered in dust but also strangely heavy. When Stella touched the first one, she felt intense anger. She put the maze into a bag and her anger went away. Stella and Brinker burned the papers down by the South Platte River.

Whether the mazes worked or the ghosts simply quieted on their own, things did calm down, and there have been no more problems with the house. The homeowners and the neighborhood animals were able to keep a safe distance from each other as the home repairs continued.

But any future owners of the house might want to keep the windows shut—just in case. Otherwise, they might start to hear tiny teeth chewing through their window screens and little claws scampering in the dark.

Union Station and the entrance to the Oxford Hotel

Lower Downtown (LoDo): Where It's Hip to Be Dead

You don't always know what might trigger a ghost to show up or how they'll behave. Some are probably as curious about us as we are about them and only want to observe. But others are more determined to interact with the living. They might wait until you're all alone, perhaps while you're trying to go to the bathroom or sleep in your fancy hotel room. You might meet one where you work, especially if you're the first to show up or the last to leave. Maybe you're never really alone anywhere . . .

Where the Specters Are Nosy, Noisy, and Ready for Bed

If you're feeling ready to tour another area of the city in search of ghosts, Lower Downtown is an excellent place to explore. From the 1950s to the 1970s, much of downtown Denver was demolished and rebuilt. However, Lower Downtown, now often called LoDo, was left intact. It wasn't torn down, but it wasn't rebuilt either. LoDo was simply ignored while the rest of downtown was redeveloped.

But a group of people saw potential in the decaying LoDo area. They got busy making plans and raising funds to create Larimer Square, which became Denver's first historic district. This preservation effort led to many other historic renovations in Lower Downtown. As you might imagine, many of the buildings in LoDo are very old, some dating back to the

1800s. You've probably figured out by now that old buildings are prime haunting spots.

The oldest hotel in Denver is the Oxford, located at 1600 Seventeenth Street, at the corner of Wazee and Seventeenth Streets. The hotel was built in 1891. At that time, so much money was made and invested along Seventeenth Street that it was called the Wall Street of the West.

Unfortunately, the financial status of the area faded over the years. By the 1970s, the hotel was in bad shape, and by the end of the decade, it was closed. But good fortune returned, and in the early 1980s, it was restored to its former glory and reopened. The Oxford, along with some permanent inhabitants who stuck around through all the changes, was ready to greet guests once again.

Sometimes, you just love a place too much to leave it, and the Oxford's ghosts are loyal to their favorite haunt. Today, the Oxford is a luxury hotel, and quiet is expected and appreciated throughout. But the ghosts obviously don't follow that unspoken rule.

Do you have a favorite room in your house? Some ghosts prefer a particular space, too. It might seem odd that one of them would choose a bathroom, but the ladies' room in the basement of the Oxford is a nice space.

However, it wasn't always a women's restroom. It contains lots of marble, and it was originally the hotel's barbershop, providing services for men only. One stubborn ghost won't stay out. He doesn't care what the sign on the door now says. And he refuses to mind his own business, too.

He doesn't show up often (thank goodness!) but when he does, it's always in the same way: peeking over a stall door, looking down on the woman inside. His face is rough, his beard is scraggly, and he has a headful of tangled curls. Judging from all this, plus the filthy condition

of his fingernails, he needs more than a barber—he needs a bath!

Once he is spotted (and usually screamed at), he goes away as quickly as he appeared. That doesn't excuse his bad behavior, but at least he's easy to get rid of.

Upstairs, there is a ballroom that is more frequently haunted. We've covered that ghosts can be seen and felt, but did you know they can sometimes be detected by smell? Hotel staff members have smelled cigar smoke in the ballroom when no one else was in there with them. Smoking has been banned in the building

for many years, but visitors have also noticed the aroma, and some have reported being able to move in and out of the boundaries of it.

The floors of the ballroom are reclaimed wood from a local bowling alley that was torn down. It's a good thing smoke is the only indication of ghosts there. Phantom gutter balls could be terrifying!

Speaking of terrifying, it's time to meet the occupants of the attic. The public isn't allowed up there, but haunted tours and ghost hunters have searched the space and have thankfully survived to share their stories.

Recording devices left in the attic overnight have picked up the voice of a little girl asking people not to feel sorry for her. A rough, threatening adult voice tells everyone they better go to sleep. Maybe this frustrated adult is why the little girl believes people might feel sorry for her.

People exploring the attic have snapped photos of lighted shapes, like ropes and orbs. Many people believe this is a sign of spiritual manifestation, a way for ghosts to appear to the living when they can't take on a human form.

Odd things can be witnessed without the aid of a camera as well. Boxes have moved across the floor on their own. A woman walking past a dusty tabletop believed she heard her friend coming up behind her, so she paused and looked back, but there was no one there. When

she glanced at the tabletop again, she saw a fresh handprint in the dust. She was certain it had not been there when she passed by the table seconds earlier. It sounds like things get creepy up in the attic. Maybe it's a good thing it is off limits.

But if you are determined to find some interactive haunting, you could always ask to stay in room 320. Don't worry if you can't remember the number. Just ask for the Murder Room. Not that you will actually get murdered there. Hardly anyone does . . .

For the most part, room 320 is quiet and nothing weird happens. When something does

happen, it's always when a man is staying in the room by himself. One of two things will occur.

The first possibility is that the guest wakes to find an uninvited man standing at the foot of his bed, yelling at him about spending time with this strange man's wife. The jealous ghost is disturbing, but so far, he hasn't carried out any physical threats.

The other potential scene in the Murder Room is far scarier. To prepare, it's a good idea to get acquainted with the room. When you open the door to room 320, the first thing you see is a small living area with old-timey furniture along with a big, modern TV. Past the

TV is a short hallway leading to the bedroom. Entering the bedroom, you see the bathroom on the left, but it's the large bed that will catch your eye.

It would not be easy to sleep with someone standing at the foot of this bed, yelling about his wife, but there are other things that might happen in room 320 to make it even more difficult. For instance, it's hard to get much rest when a ghost keeps flipping the bathroom lights on and off. So annoying.

But things could get much, much worse. Occasionally, the covers will lift off the guest who is trying to sleep under them. And then, the mattress will shift and groan as someone climbs into the bed next to the guest— someone unseen!

Sweet dreams with an invisible bedmate? Not likely.

As far as who was murdered in room 320 to earn it the nickname of the Murder Room, no one seems to know. Perhaps no one who knew lived to tell the tale.

So would you like to reserve room 320 at the Oxford when you're in Denver overnight? You can tell all your friends you stayed in the Murder Room—if you live to check out, that is.

A GHOST NEEDS HER BEAUTY REST
(AND NO VISITS FROM HER SISTER!)

Heading southwest on Seventeenth Street, away from Union Station, takes us to our next spirit hangout. A right on Market Street reveals what used to be the Aveda Academy at 1650 Market Street.

When this salon and spa was open, its resident ghost was fairly easygoing, occasionally opening the dryer or moving things about. But if you interrupted her too early in the morning, she would make her displeasure well known. This spirit did not like surprises.

If someone bustled through the doors early in the morning, hustling in a flurry instead of entering the space calmly, the ghost would react with equal chaos. She would knock things over—and not always small things. This spirit could topple heavy salon chairs when her peace was disrupted.

She really showed her sass at night when the cleaning crew was present. Though she

coexisted nicely with the daytime occupants of the space most of the time, she did not like people coming in after hours. It's possible she felt like a guardian of the Aveda Academy and was trying to protect it.

A woman on the cleaning crew brought her teenage daughter to work with her one night. She quit because her daughter was physically pushed around by someone they couldn't see. The girl was in a back area, where customers were not allowed, near the cash, computers, and other sensitive items. The ghost may have acted out because she perceived the girl as a threat.

Another woman quit after the ghost stole one of her shoes. She arrived for work one evening and placed her shoes by the front door. A while later, she found her shoes had both been thrown across the room. She replaced them neatly by the front door. After she was finished cleaning, one shoe had been tossed away from the door again, and the other was nowhere to be found.

The manager of the cleaning crew asked to send a medium (psychic) to the business to find out what was going on and perhaps help a restless spirit pass to the other side. The owner of the Aveda Academy agreed on the condition that the ghost not be forced to leave. She had grown accustomed to having her around.

When the medium arrived, the ghost greeted her proudly by saying, "Hello, my name is Josephine. You are here to see me!"

Josephine informed the medium she had lived in the early 1900s, but she didn't seem to be aware she was no longer alive. When the medium asked her about taking the woman's shoe, Josephine admitted she had done it. She said the woman reminded her of her sister. Josephine went on to explain she never liked her sister, and she had no intention of giving her shoe back. Where does a ghost permanently hide a shoe? Maybe it's lodged forever in the thin space between this world and the spirit world. Maybe it landed in another building somewhere, a mystery never to be solved by those who found it. One unclaimed shoe, eternally separated from its mate, all because a pair of siblings couldn't get along, not even in the afterlife.

At the time of this writing, 1650 Market Street is available for a new business, so Josephine has the place all to herself. If you're in the area, maybe you should stop by for a visit. She's probably lonely. As long as you remember to enter Josephine's realm gently during the day, hopefully she'll be happy to see you. No promises about after-hours visits, or your shoes if you remind her of her sister.

THE FLASHY SPIRIT OF A HERO

Further up Market Street is a building that was once home to the restaurant and bar called the Soiled Dove. It was also the haunt of a

friendlier ghost than most we've met so far in Denver. In fact, this ghost may have been an actual lifesaver.

One night, two young women were the last employees to leave the Soiled Dove. One had parked her car in the alley behind the business,

and the other was parked down the street. The two coworkers went about the normal duties of closing down: cleaning, putting up the chairs, turning off all the lights—all things they had done many nights before.

When they had the place clean and ready for the next day, the women said goodbye. One headed for the back door and the other for the front. The agreement was they would each lock the door behind them, securing the location for the night.

Before they made their way outside, the still darkness of the bar erupted in flashing lights. The lights around the stage area spontaneously began to flash red. Both women were sure they had turned off all the lights. How was this happening? Was there some sort of electrical problem?

With their questioning faces partially lit by the flashing lights, they wondered if they had somehow missed a switch. The stage wasn't large, but it was big enough for bands to play live music. Around the edge were multicolored lights to enhance the performances. One of the women went to recheck the switches. The lights were definitely all turned off. She turned them on and then back off again to be sure the switches were fully in the off positions.

The women chatted briefly about how strange it was but agreed that all seemed well now. Once again, they said goodbye and headed for opposite doors. But just like before, the lights started flashing before they could leave. Red! Red! Red!

This time, the woman who was headed for the alley felt a tingling sensation at the base of her skull. Her stomach went cold, and she was overcome with a strong sense of dread. She was positive someone was trying to tell her something. The lights weren't malfunctioning. They were flashing a warning.

The lights did not flash again, but both women now felt uneasy about leaving the way they had originally planned. They agreed it would be better if they walked together to the car owned by the woman who parked down the street, and she would drive her friend back to the alley.

They both exited through the front door and walked in silence. Safely inside the car, they drove along Twentieth Street and turned into the alley between Market Street and Blake Street. It was an exceptionally dark night, and when the car first turned into the alley, the headlights shone on the waiting car. But soon, as the car continued into the alley, something else was illuminated—a sight that would chill the women to their cores.

Because the Soiled Dove's rear door was recessed, anyone exiting through it wouldn't be able to see the surrounding area before stepping past the short walls that framed the door and fully into the alley. There was more waiting outside the Soiled Dove's back exit than a car that night. Two men stood with their backs pressed against the wall on either side of the exit, waiting for the woman to come out, knowing she wouldn't see them until it was too late for her to turn around and run back inside.

As the headlights from the approaching car washed over them and the two men realized

they'd been seen, they took off running down the alley in the opposite direction.

The Soiled Dove had never shown any signs of being haunted before, nor did it show any after that night. But when it really mattered for the young woman who had parked in the alley, a ghost gathered enough power to deliver the message.

It's impossible to say for sure what the two men intended, but innocent people don't usually try to hide their presence near back doors or turn and run away as soon as they are spotted.

A ghost doesn't often get to be the hero in a story, but the one who flashed the red lights at the Soiled Dove that night surely seems to have earned the honor.

Our tour ends here, but there is much more to explore in the great city of Denver. It's no wonder the residents of this city are proud to call Denver home. Just remember, for some, it is an eternal home. You may be walking new sidewalks right alongside some very old residents—some you'll never see and perhaps others you'll wish you hadn't.

Note: Some names may have been changed out of concern for the privacy of the people who shared personal accounts in the ghost stories included, but the locations and events have been recorded as accurately as possible. Historical names of homes and mansions have not been changed.

Shelli Timmons writes for kids of all ages. After many years working with numbers, she realized she liked letters a whole lot more, so she stepped away from the world of finance and entered the realm of stories. She loves old houses and buildings, and is always open to sharing space with a ghost or two. She currently lives in Central Texas in a house much newer than she'd prefer, with an equal number of people and dogs. Check out her website, shellicornelison.net and follow Shelli on Twitter at @Shelltex.

Check out some of the other Spooky America titles available now!

Spooky America was adapted from the creeptastic Haunted America series for adults. Haunted America explores historical haunts in cities and regions across America. Each book chronicles both the widely known and less-familiar history behind local ghosts and other unexplained mysteries. Here's more from the original *The Haunted Heart of Denver* author Kevin Pharris:

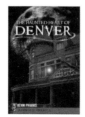
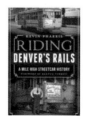

See more on Instagram @treasureboxtours.